# 50 Winter Feast Recipes for Home

By: Kelly Johnson

# Table of Contents

- Roasted Butternut Squash Soup
- Beef Stew with Root Vegetables
- Herb-Roasted Turkey with Cranberry Sauce
- Garlic Mashed Potatoes
- Creamy Mushroom Risotto
- Honey Glazed Ham
- Baked Macaroni and Cheese
- Spiced Pumpkin Pie
- Braised Lamb Shanks
- Apple Walnut Salad with Maple Dressing
- Slow Cooker Chicken Noodle Soup
- Roasted Brussels Sprouts with Balsamic Glaze
- Beef and Barley Stew
- Spinach and Feta Stuffed Chicken Breast
- Classic French Onion Soup
- Glazed Carrots with Thyme
- Pork Tenderloin with Apples and Onions
- Sweet Potato Casserole with Marshmallow Topping
- Creamy Wild Rice Soup
- Roast Duck with Orange Sauce
- Cranberry Pecan Stuffing
- Baked Brie with Cranberry Compote
- Beef Wellington
- Creamy Cauliflower Gratin
- Pear and Gorgonzola Salad
- Chicken Pot Pie
- Buttermilk Biscuits
- Roasted Garlic Mashed Cauliflower
- Maple Glazed Salmon
- Vegetarian Shepherd's Pie
- Mulled Wine
- Roasted Chestnuts
- Winter Citrus Salad
- Beef Bourguignon
- Pumpkin Cheesecake

- Cornbread Stuffing
- Herb Crusted Rack of Lamb
- Glazed Sweet Potatoes
- Mushroom Wellington
- Cranberry Orange Bread
- Sausage and Apple Stuffed Acorn Squash
- Creamy Polenta
- Roasted Vegetable Lasagna
- Cinnamon Baked Apples
- Potato Leek Soup
- Stuffed Pork Tenderloin with Cranberry Sauce
- Roasted Beet Salad with Goat Cheese
- Garlic and Herb Roasted Prime Rib
- Winter Vegetable Tian
- Chocolate Peppermint Trifle

**Roasted Butternut Squash Soup**

Ingredients:

- 1 medium-sized butternut squash, peeled, seeded, and cubed
- 1 onion, chopped
- 2 cloves garlic, minced
- 2 tablespoons olive oil
- 4 cups vegetable or chicken broth
- 1 teaspoon ground cumin
- 1/2 teaspoon ground cinnamon
- Salt and pepper to taste
- Optional toppings: chopped fresh herbs (such as parsley or chives), a dollop of sour cream or Greek yogurt, toasted pumpkin seeds, croutons

Instructions:

Preheat your oven to 400°F (200°C).
Place the cubed butternut squash on a baking sheet lined with parchment paper. Drizzle with 1 tablespoon of olive oil and season with salt and pepper. Toss to coat evenly.
Roast the squash in the preheated oven for about 25-30 minutes, or until tender and lightly caramelized.
In a large pot, heat the remaining 1 tablespoon of olive oil over medium heat. Add the chopped onion and cook until softened, about 5 minutes. Add the minced garlic and cook for another minute.
Add the roasted butternut squash to the pot, along with the vegetable or chicken broth, ground cumin, and ground cinnamon. Bring the mixture to a simmer.
Let the soup simmer for about 15 minutes to allow the flavors to meld together.
Using an immersion blender or regular blender, puree the soup until smooth. Be careful when blending hot liquids.
Season the soup with additional salt and pepper to taste.
Serve the soup hot, garnished with your choice of toppings such as chopped fresh herbs, a dollop of sour cream or Greek yogurt, toasted pumpkin seeds, or croutons.

Enjoy your delicious homemade Roasted Butternut Squash Soup!

**Beef Stew with Root Vegetables**

Ingredients:

- 2 pounds (about 900g) beef chuck roast, cut into bite-sized pieces
- 2 tablespoons all-purpose flour
- Salt and pepper to taste
- 2 tablespoons olive oil
- 1 large onion, chopped
- 3 cloves garlic, minced
- 4 cups beef broth
- 2 tablespoons tomato paste
- 1 tablespoon Worcestershire sauce
- 1 teaspoon dried thyme
- 2 bay leaves
- 4 carrots, peeled and cut into chunks
- 4 medium potatoes, peeled and cut into chunks
- 2 parsnips, peeled and cut into chunks
- 2 celery stalks, chopped
- Chopped fresh parsley for garnish (optional)

Instructions:

In a large bowl, toss the beef pieces with the flour, salt, and pepper until well coated.

Heat the olive oil in a large pot or Dutch oven over medium-high heat. Add the beef in batches and brown on all sides. Transfer the browned beef to a plate and set aside.

In the same pot, add the chopped onion and cook until softened, about 5 minutes. Add the minced garlic and cook for another minute.

Return the browned beef to the pot. Add the beef broth, tomato paste, Worcestershire sauce, dried thyme, and bay leaves. Stir to combine.

Bring the stew to a simmer, then reduce the heat to low. Cover and let simmer for 1 to 1 1/2 hours, or until the beef is tender.

Add the carrots, potatoes, parsnips, and celery to the pot. Stir to combine.

Cover and simmer for an additional 30 minutes, or until the vegetables are tender and the flavors have melded together.

Taste and adjust the seasoning with salt and pepper if needed.

Remove the bay leaves from the stew before serving.

Serve the beef stew hot, garnished with chopped fresh parsley if desired.

Enjoy your comforting beef stew with root vegetables!

**Herb-Roasted Turkey with Cranberry Sauce**

Ingredients:

- 1 whole turkey (about 12-15 pounds)
- 1/2 cup unsalted butter, softened
- 2 tablespoons chopped fresh herbs (such as rosemary, thyme, and sage)
- Salt and pepper to taste
- 1 onion, quartered
- 1 lemon, quartered
- 4 cloves garlic, smashed
- 2 cups chicken or turkey broth
- Kitchen twine

Instructions:

Preheat your oven to 325°F (165°C).

Remove the giblets and neck from the turkey cavity and pat the turkey dry with paper towels.

In a small bowl, mix together the softened butter, chopped fresh herbs, salt, and pepper.

Carefully loosen the skin of the turkey breast by gently sliding your fingers underneath the skin, being careful not to tear it.

Spread half of the herb butter mixture under the skin of the turkey breast, distributing it as evenly as possible.

Rub the remaining herb butter mixture over the outside of the turkey.

Stuff the turkey cavity with the quartered onion, lemon, and smashed garlic cloves.

Tie the legs together with kitchen twine and tuck the wing tips under the body of the turkey.

Place the turkey on a roasting rack set inside a roasting pan.

Pour the chicken or turkey broth into the bottom of the roasting pan.

Roast the turkey in the preheated oven, basting every 30 minutes with the pan juices, until the internal temperature reaches 165°F (74°C) in the thickest part of the thigh, about 3 to 4 hours for a 12-15 pound turkey.

If the turkey begins to brown too quickly, tent it loosely with aluminum foil.

Once cooked, remove the turkey from the oven and let it rest for 20-30 minutes before carving.

Cranberry Sauce:

Ingredients:

- 1 cup granulated sugar
- 1 cup water
- 12 ounces fresh cranberries

Instructions:

In a saucepan, combine the sugar and water. Bring to a boil over medium heat, stirring until the sugar is dissolved.
Add the fresh cranberries to the saucepan and return to a boil.
Reduce the heat to medium-low and simmer the cranberries, stirring occasionally, until they burst and the sauce thickens, about 10-15 minutes.
Remove the cranberry sauce from the heat and let it cool to room temperature before serving.

Serving:

Slice the herb-roasted turkey and serve it with the cranberry sauce on the side. You can also serve it with your favorite sides like mashed potatoes, stuffing, roasted vegetables, and gravy.

Enjoy your delicious herb-roasted turkey with cranberry sauce!

**Garlic Mashed Potatoes**

Ingredients:

- 2 pounds (about 900g) potatoes (such as Yukon Gold or Russet), peeled and cut into chunks
- 4 cloves garlic, peeled
- 1/2 cup (120ml) milk or cream
- 4 tablespoons (about 55g) unsalted butter
- Salt and pepper to taste
- Chopped fresh parsley for garnish (optional)

Instructions:

Place the potato chunks and garlic cloves in a large pot and cover them with cold water. Add a generous pinch of salt to the water.
Bring the water to a boil over high heat, then reduce the heat to medium-low and let the potatoes simmer until they are fork-tender, about 15-20 minutes.
While the potatoes are cooking, heat the milk or cream and butter in a small saucepan over low heat until the butter is melted. Keep warm.
Once the potatoes are cooked, drain them in a colander and return them to the pot.
Using a potato masher or a fork, mash the potatoes and garlic until they reach your desired consistency. Some people prefer smooth mashed potatoes, while others like them slightly chunky.
Gradually pour the warm milk or cream mixture into the mashed potatoes, stirring until smooth and creamy. You may not need to use all of the milk/cream mixture, so add it gradually until you reach your desired consistency.
Season the mashed potatoes with salt and pepper to taste, adjusting as needed.
Transfer the mashed potatoes to a serving dish and garnish with chopped fresh parsley, if desired.
Serve the garlic mashed potatoes hot alongside your favorite main dishes.

Enjoy your creamy and flavorful garlic mashed potatoes!

**Creamy Mushroom Risotto**

Ingredients:

- 1 cup Arborio rice
- 4 cups chicken or vegetable broth
- 2 tablespoons olive oil
- 2 tablespoons butter
- 1 onion, finely chopped
- 2 cloves garlic, minced
- 8 ounces (about 225g) mushrooms (such as cremini or button), sliced
- 1/2 cup dry white wine (optional)
- 1/2 cup grated Parmesan cheese
- Salt and pepper to taste
- Chopped fresh parsley for garnish (optional)

Instructions:

In a saucepan, heat the chicken or vegetable broth over medium heat until it simmers. Keep it warm on the stove.
In a large skillet or saucepan, heat the olive oil and butter over medium heat.
Add the chopped onion to the skillet and cook until softened, about 5 minutes.
Add the minced garlic to the skillet and cook for another minute, until fragrant.
Add the sliced mushrooms to the skillet and cook until they are softened and browned, about 5-7 minutes.
Add the Arborio rice to the skillet and stir to coat it with the oil, butter, and mushroom mixture. Cook for 1-2 minutes until the rice is lightly toasted.
If using, pour in the white wine and stir until it is absorbed by the rice.
Begin adding the warm broth to the skillet, one ladleful at a time, stirring constantly and allowing each addition of broth to be absorbed before adding more. This process will take about 20-25 minutes, and the risotto should be creamy and the rice tender but still slightly firm to the bite (al dente).
Once all the broth has been added and the risotto is creamy and cooked to your liking, remove the skillet from the heat.
Stir in the grated Parmesan cheese until it is melted and well combined with the risotto.
Season the mushroom risotto with salt and pepper to taste.
Garnish with chopped fresh parsley, if desired, before serving.

Enjoy your creamy mushroom risotto as a satisfying and comforting meal!

**Honey Glazed Ham**

Ingredients:

- 1 fully cooked bone-in ham (about 8-10 pounds)
- 1/2 cup honey
- 1/4 cup brown sugar
- 2 tablespoons Dijon mustard
- 2 tablespoons apple cider vinegar
- 1 teaspoon ground cinnamon
- 1/2 teaspoon ground cloves
- Whole cloves for garnish (optional)
- Pineapple rings for garnish (optional)
- Maraschino cherries for garnish (optional)

Instructions:

Preheat your oven to 325°F (165°C).
Remove the ham from its packaging and place it in a roasting pan, cut side down. Score the surface of the ham in a diamond pattern with a sharp knife, making cuts about 1/4 inch deep.
In a small saucepan, combine the honey, brown sugar, Dijon mustard, apple cider vinegar, ground cinnamon, and ground cloves. Heat the mixture over medium heat, stirring constantly, until the sugar is dissolved and the glaze is smooth, about 5 minutes.
Brush about half of the glaze over the surface of the ham, making sure to get it into the scored cuts.
If desired, insert whole cloves into the ham at the intersections of the scored cuts for added flavor and decoration.
Cover the ham loosely with aluminum foil and place it in the preheated oven.
Bake the ham for about 10-15 minutes per pound, or until heated through, basting with the remaining glaze every 30 minutes.
About 30 minutes before the ham is done, you can arrange pineapple rings and maraschino cherries on top of the ham for added flavor and presentation. Secure them with toothpicks if necessary.
Once the ham is heated through and nicely glazed, remove it from the oven and let it rest for 10-15 minutes before slicing.

Serve your honey glazed ham warm, and enjoy it as the centerpiece of your meal!

**Baked Macaroni and Cheese**

Ingredients:

- 8 ounces (about 225g) elbow macaroni or any pasta shape of your choice
- 2 tablespoons butter
- 2 tablespoons all-purpose flour
- 2 cups milk
- 2 cups shredded cheese (such as cheddar, mozzarella, or a combination)
- 1/2 teaspoon salt
- 1/4 teaspoon black pepper
- 1/4 teaspoon paprika (optional)
- 1/4 cup breadcrumbs (optional)
- Chopped fresh parsley for garnish (optional)

Instructions:

Preheat your oven to 350°F (175°C). Grease a baking dish with butter or cooking spray.
Cook the macaroni according to the package instructions until it is al dente. Drain and set aside.
In a medium saucepan, melt the butter over medium heat.
Stir in the flour and cook, stirring constantly, for 1-2 minutes to make a roux.
Gradually whisk in the milk, stirring constantly to prevent lumps from forming.
Cook the sauce, stirring frequently, until it thickens and coats the back of a spoon, about 5-7 minutes.
Remove the saucepan from the heat and stir in the shredded cheese until it is melted and the sauce is smooth.
Season the cheese sauce with salt, pepper, and paprika, if using.
Add the cooked macaroni to the cheese sauce and stir until the pasta is evenly coated.
Pour the macaroni and cheese mixture into the prepared baking dish, spreading it out evenly.
If desired, sprinkle breadcrumbs over the top of the macaroni and cheese for added texture.
Bake the macaroni and cheese in the preheated oven for 20-25 minutes, or until the top is golden brown and the cheese is bubbly.
Remove the baking dish from the oven and let the macaroni and cheese cool for a few minutes before serving.
Garnish with chopped fresh parsley, if desired, before serving.

Serve your baked macaroni and cheese hot as a delicious and comforting side dish or main course. Enjoy!

**Spiced Pumpkin Pie**

Ingredients:

For the pie crust:

- 1 1/4 cups all-purpose flour
- 1/2 teaspoon salt
- 1/2 teaspoon granulated sugar
- 1/2 cup (1 stick) unsalted butter, cold and cut into small pieces
- 3-4 tablespoons ice water

For the filling:

- 1 (15-ounce) can pumpkin puree (not pumpkin pie filling)
- 3/4 cup granulated sugar
- 2 large eggs
- 1 teaspoon ground cinnamon
- 1/2 teaspoon ground ginger
- 1/4 teaspoon ground nutmeg
- 1/4 teaspoon ground cloves
- 1/2 teaspoon salt
- 1 cup evaporated milk or half-and-half

Instructions:

For the pie crust:

In a large mixing bowl, combine the flour, salt, and sugar.
Add the cold butter pieces to the flour mixture and use a pastry cutter or your fingers to cut the butter into the flour until the mixture resembles coarse crumbs.
Gradually add the ice water, 1 tablespoon at a time, mixing with a fork until the dough just begins to come together.
Gather the dough into a ball, flatten it into a disk, wrap it in plastic wrap, and refrigerate for at least 30 minutes.

For the filling:

Preheat your oven to 425°F (220°C).
In a large mixing bowl, whisk together the pumpkin puree, sugar, eggs, cinnamon, ginger, nutmeg, cloves, and salt until well combined.
Gradually stir in the evaporated milk or half-and-half until the mixture is smooth and uniform.

Assembling the pie:

Roll out the chilled pie dough on a lightly floured surface into a circle about 12 inches in diameter.
Carefully transfer the rolled-out dough to a 9-inch pie dish, pressing it gently into the bottom and up the sides of the dish. Trim any excess dough and crimp the edges as desired.
Pour the pumpkin filling into the prepared pie crust.
Place the pie in the preheated oven and bake at 425°F (220°C) for 15 minutes.
Reduce the oven temperature to 350°F (175°C) and continue baking for an additional 45-50 minutes, or until the filling is set and the crust is golden brown.
Remove the pie from the oven and let it cool completely on a wire rack before serving.
Serve the spiced pumpkin pie at room temperature or chilled, topped with whipped cream if desired.

Enjoy your homemade spiced pumpkin pie, a delicious and comforting dessert for any occasion!

**Braised Lamb Shanks**

Ingredients:

- 4 lamb shanks
- Salt and pepper to taste
- 2 tablespoons olive oil
- 1 onion, chopped
- 2 carrots, chopped
- 2 stalks celery, chopped
- 4 cloves garlic, minced
- 1 cup red wine
- 2 cups beef or chicken broth
- 2 sprigs fresh rosemary
- 2 sprigs fresh thyme
- 2 bay leaves
- 1 can (14 ounces) diced tomatoes
- 2 tablespoons tomato paste
- 1 tablespoon Worcestershire sauce
- Chopped fresh parsley for garnish (optional)

Instructions:

Preheat your oven to 325°F (160°C).
Season the lamb shanks generously with salt and pepper.
In a large Dutch oven or oven-safe pot, heat the olive oil over medium-high heat. Add the lamb shanks to the pot and cook until they are browned on all sides, about 4-5 minutes per side. Remove the lamb shanks from the pot and set aside.
In the same pot, add the chopped onion, carrots, and celery. Cook until the vegetables are softened, about 5 minutes.
Add the minced garlic to the pot and cook for another minute, until fragrant.
Pour in the red wine and deglaze the pot, scraping up any browned bits from the bottom with a wooden spoon.
Add the beef or chicken broth, fresh rosemary, thyme, bay leaves, diced tomatoes, tomato paste, and Worcestershire sauce to the pot. Stir to combine.
Return the lamb shanks to the pot, nestling them into the liquid and vegetables.
Cover the pot with a lid and transfer it to the preheated oven.
Braise the lamb shanks in the oven for 2-2 1/2 hours, or until the meat is tender and falling off the bone.

Once the lamb shanks are done, remove them from the oven and transfer them to a serving dish.

Skim off any excess fat from the cooking liquid and discard the herb sprigs and bay leaves.

If desired, you can thicken the cooking liquid into a sauce by simmering it on the stovetop over medium heat until it has reduced slightly.

Serve the lamb shanks hot, garnished with chopped fresh parsley if desired, and with the sauce spooned over the top.

Enjoy your flavorful and tender braised lamb shanks!

**Apple Walnut Salad with Maple Dressing**

Ingredients:

For the salad:

- 6 cups mixed salad greens (such as baby spinach, arugula, and leaf lettuce)
- 2 apples, cored and thinly sliced (use your favorite variety)
- 1/2 cup walnuts, chopped
- 1/4 cup dried cranberries or raisins
- 1/4 cup crumbled feta cheese (optional)

For the maple dressing:

- 1/4 cup olive oil
- 2 tablespoons apple cider vinegar
- 2 tablespoons pure maple syrup
- 1 tablespoon Dijon mustard
- Salt and pepper to taste

Instructions:

In a large salad bowl, combine the mixed salad greens, sliced apples, chopped walnuts, dried cranberries or raisins, and crumbled feta cheese (if using). Toss gently to combine.

In a small bowl or jar, whisk together the olive oil, apple cider vinegar, maple syrup, Dijon mustard, salt, and pepper until emulsified. Alternatively, you can shake the ingredients together in a jar with a tight-fitting lid.

Drizzle the maple dressing over the salad just before serving, tossing gently to coat all the ingredients evenly.

Serve the apple walnut salad immediately as a refreshing side dish or light meal. Optionally, you can garnish the salad with additional chopped walnuts or crumbled feta cheese before serving.

Enjoy the crisp, refreshing flavors of this Apple Walnut Salad with Maple Dressing! It's perfect for a light lunch or as a side dish for dinner.

**Slow Cooker Chicken Noodle Soup**

Ingredients:

- 1 pound boneless, skinless chicken breasts or thighs
- 6 cups chicken broth
- 2 carrots, sliced
- 2 celery stalks, sliced
- 1 onion, chopped
- 3 cloves garlic, minced
- 1 teaspoon dried thyme
- 1 teaspoon dried parsley
- 1/2 teaspoon dried rosemary
- 1 bay leaf
- Salt and pepper to taste
- 2 cups uncooked egg noodles
- Fresh parsley for garnish (optional)

Instructions:

Place the chicken breasts or thighs in the bottom of your slow cooker.
Add the sliced carrots, sliced celery, chopped onion, minced garlic, dried thyme, dried parsley, dried rosemary, bay leaf, salt, and pepper on top of the chicken.
Pour the chicken broth over the ingredients in the slow cooker.
Cover and cook on low heat for 6-8 hours or on high heat for 3-4 hours, until the chicken is cooked through and vegetables are tender.
Remove the cooked chicken from the slow cooker and shred it using two forks.
Return the shredded chicken to the slow cooker.
Stir in the uncooked egg noodles.
Cover and cook on high heat for an additional 15-20 minutes, or until the noodles are tender.
Taste and adjust seasoning with salt and pepper if needed.
Remove the bay leaf before serving.
Ladle the chicken noodle soup into bowls and garnish with fresh parsley if desired.
Serve hot and enjoy the comforting and delicious slow cooker chicken noodle soup!

Feel free to customize this recipe by adding your favorite vegetables or herbs. It's a versatile dish that's sure to warm you up on a cold day!

**Roasted Brussels Sprouts with Balsamic Glaze**

Ingredients:

- 1 pound Brussels sprouts, trimmed and halved
- 2 tablespoons olive oil
- Salt and pepper to taste
- 2 tablespoons balsamic vinegar
- 1 tablespoon honey or maple syrup (optional)
- 1-2 cloves garlic, minced (optional)
- Grated Parmesan cheese for garnish (optional)

Instructions:

Preheat your oven to 400°F (200°C).
In a large mixing bowl, toss the halved Brussels sprouts with olive oil until they are evenly coated.
Season the Brussels sprouts with salt and pepper to taste.
Arrange the Brussels sprouts in a single layer on a baking sheet lined with parchment paper or aluminum foil, cut side down.
Roast the Brussels sprouts in the preheated oven for 20-25 minutes, or until they are tender and caramelized, stirring halfway through cooking.
While the Brussels sprouts are roasting, prepare the balsamic glaze. In a small saucepan, combine the balsamic vinegar, honey or maple syrup (if using), and minced garlic (if using). Bring the mixture to a simmer over medium heat, then reduce the heat to low and let it simmer gently for 5-7 minutes, or until it has thickened slightly.
Once the Brussels sprouts are done roasting, transfer them to a serving dish.
Drizzle the balsamic glaze over the roasted Brussels sprouts.
If desired, garnish with grated Parmesan cheese for added flavor.
Serve the roasted Brussels sprouts with balsamic glaze hot as a delicious side dish.

Enjoy the delicious flavor of roasted Brussels sprouts with balsamic glaze! It's a perfect addition to any meal.

**Beef and Barley Stew**

Ingredients:

- 1 pound stewing beef, cut into bite-sized pieces
- 2 tablespoons olive oil
- 1 onion, chopped
- 2 carrots, chopped
- 2 celery stalks, chopped
- 2 cloves garlic, minced
- 1/2 cup pearl barley, rinsed
- 4 cups beef broth
- 1 can (14.5 ounces) diced tomatoes
- 1 teaspoon dried thyme
- 1 teaspoon dried rosemary
- Salt and pepper to taste
- Chopped fresh parsley for garnish (optional)

Instructions:

In a large pot or Dutch oven, heat the olive oil over medium-high heat.
Add the stewing beef to the pot and cook until browned on all sides, about 5-7 minutes. Remove the beef from the pot and set aside.
In the same pot, add the chopped onion, carrots, and celery. Cook until the vegetables are softened, about 5 minutes.
Add the minced garlic to the pot and cook for another minute, until fragrant.
Return the browned beef to the pot. Add the rinsed pearl barley, beef broth, diced tomatoes (with their juices), dried thyme, dried rosemary, salt, and pepper. Stir to combine.
Bring the stew to a simmer, then reduce the heat to low. Cover and let simmer for about 1 hour, stirring occasionally, or until the beef is tender and the barley is cooked.
Taste and adjust seasoning with salt and pepper if needed.
Once the stew is done cooking, remove it from the heat and let it sit for a few minutes before serving.
Ladle the beef and barley stew into bowls and garnish with chopped fresh parsley if desired.
Serve hot and enjoy the hearty and comforting flavors of this delicious stew!

This beef and barley stew is perfect for a cozy dinner at home. It's packed with protein, fiber, and flavor, making it a satisfying meal for any occasion.

**Spinach and Feta Stuffed Chicken Breast**

Ingredients:

- 4 boneless, skinless chicken breasts
- Salt and pepper to taste
- 2 cups fresh spinach leaves
- 1/2 cup crumbled feta cheese
- 2 cloves garlic, minced
- 1 tablespoon olive oil
- 1 tablespoon Italian seasoning
- Toothpicks or kitchen twine (optional)
- Lemon wedges for serving (optional)

Instructions:

Preheat your oven to 375°F (190°C).

Place each chicken breast between two sheets of plastic wrap or parchment paper. Use a meat mallet or rolling pin to pound the chicken breasts to an even thickness, about 1/2 inch thick. Season both sides of the chicken breasts with salt and pepper.

In a skillet, heat the olive oil over medium heat. Add the minced garlic and cook for about 1 minute, until fragrant.

Add the fresh spinach leaves to the skillet and cook, stirring frequently, until wilted, about 2-3 minutes. Remove the skillet from the heat.

In a mixing bowl, combine the cooked spinach with the crumbled feta cheese. Stir to combine.

Place a spoonful of the spinach and feta mixture onto each chicken breast. Roll up the chicken breasts, starting from the short end, and secure with toothpicks or kitchen twine if necessary to hold the filling inside.

Place the stuffed chicken breasts in a baking dish. Drizzle with a little olive oil and sprinkle with Italian seasoning.

Bake in the preheated oven for 25-30 minutes, or until the chicken is cooked through and reaches an internal temperature of 165°F (74°C).

Remove the stuffed chicken breasts from the oven and let them rest for a few minutes before serving.

Optionally, garnish the stuffed chicken breasts with lemon wedges before serving for a burst of freshness.

Serve hot and enjoy your delicious spinach and feta stuffed chicken breast!

This dish pairs well with a variety of side dishes, such as roasted vegetables, mashed potatoes, or a simple green salad. It's sure to impress your family and guests with its delicious flavors and elegant presentation.

**Classic French Onion Soup**

Ingredients:

- 4 large onions, thinly sliced
- 2 tablespoons butter
- 2 tablespoons olive oil
- 4 cloves garlic, minced
- 1 teaspoon granulated sugar
- 1/2 cup dry white wine (optional)
- 6 cups beef broth
- 2 sprigs fresh thyme
- 1 bay leaf
- Salt and pepper to taste
- Baguette or French bread, sliced
- Gruyère cheese, grated
- Fresh parsley for garnish (optional)

Instructions:

In a large pot or Dutch oven, melt the butter with the olive oil over medium heat. Add the thinly sliced onions to the pot and cook, stirring occasionally, until they are caramelized and golden brown, about 30-40 minutes. Stir in the minced garlic and cook for an additional 1-2 minutes.
Sprinkle the sugar over the caramelized onions and stir to combine. This will help enhance the caramelization process.
If using, pour in the dry white wine to deglaze the pot, scraping up any browned bits from the bottom with a wooden spoon. Cook for a few minutes until the wine has reduced slightly.
Add the beef broth, fresh thyme sprigs, and bay leaf to the pot. Season with salt and pepper to taste. Bring the soup to a simmer and let it cook for about 20-30 minutes to allow the flavors to meld together.
While the soup is simmering, preheat your oven's broiler.
Place the sliced baguette or French bread on a baking sheet and toast it under the broiler until golden brown on both sides.
Once the soup is ready, discard the thyme sprigs and bay leaf.
Ladle the soup into oven-safe bowls. Place a few slices of toasted bread on top of each bowl of soup.
Sprinkle a generous amount of grated Gruyère cheese over the bread slices, covering them completely.

Place the soup bowls under the broiler and broil for 2-3 minutes, or until the cheese is melted and bubbly and starts to brown.
Carefully remove the soup bowls from the oven using oven mitts.
Garnish the French onion soup with fresh parsley if desired, and serve hot.

Enjoy this classic French onion soup with its rich, savory broth, caramelized onions, and gooey melted cheese—it's the perfect comfort food for any occasion!

**Glazed Carrots with Thyme**

Ingredients:

- 1 pound carrots, peeled and sliced into rounds or sticks
- 2 tablespoons butter
- 2 tablespoons honey or maple syrup
- 1 teaspoon fresh thyme leaves
- Salt and pepper to taste
- Chopped fresh parsley for garnish (optional)

Instructions:

In a large skillet or saucepan, melt the butter over medium heat.
Add the sliced carrots to the skillet and cook, stirring occasionally, for about 5 minutes, until they start to soften.
Stir in the honey or maple syrup, fresh thyme leaves, salt, and pepper to taste.
Continue cooking the carrots, stirring frequently, for another 5-7 minutes, or until they are tender and glazed, and the sauce has thickened slightly.
Taste and adjust seasoning with salt and pepper if needed.
Once the carrots are done cooking, remove the skillet from the heat.
Transfer the glazed carrots to a serving dish and garnish with chopped fresh parsley if desired.
Serve hot as a delicious and flavorful side dish.

These glazed carrots with thyme are perfect for holidays, dinner parties, or any time you want to add a touch of sweetness and herbaceous flavor to your meal. Enjoy!

**Pork Tenderloin with Apples and Onions**

Ingredients:

- 1 pork tenderloin (about 1 to 1 1/2 pounds)
- Salt and pepper to taste
- 2 tablespoons olive oil
- 2 tablespoons butter
- 2 apples, cored and sliced (such as Granny Smith or Honeycrisp)
- 1 large onion, thinly sliced
- 2 cloves garlic, minced
- 1/2 cup apple cider or apple juice
- 1/2 cup chicken broth or vegetable broth
- 2 tablespoons Dijon mustard
- 2 tablespoons maple syrup or honey
- 1 teaspoon dried thyme (or 1 tablespoon fresh thyme leaves)
- Chopped fresh parsley for garnish (optional)

Instructions:

Preheat your oven to 375°F (190°C).
Season the pork tenderloin with salt and pepper on all sides.
In a large oven-safe skillet or roasting pan, heat the olive oil over medium-high heat.
Add the pork tenderloin to the skillet and sear it on all sides until browned, about 2-3 minutes per side. Remove the pork from the skillet and set it aside.
In the same skillet, melt the butter over medium heat. Add the sliced apples and onions to the skillet and cook, stirring occasionally, until they start to soften, about 5 minutes.
Add the minced garlic to the skillet and cook for another minute, until fragrant.
Stir in the apple cider or apple juice, chicken broth or vegetable broth, Dijon mustard, maple syrup or honey, and dried thyme. Bring the mixture to a simmer.
Return the pork tenderloin to the skillet, nestling it among the apples and onions.
Transfer the skillet to the preheated oven and roast the pork tenderloin for 15-20 minutes, or until it reaches an internal temperature of 145°F (63°C) for medium rare, or 160°F (71°C) for medium, as measured with a meat thermometer inserted into the thickest part of the pork.
Once the pork is done cooking, remove the skillet from the oven and let the pork rest for a few minutes before slicing.

Slice the pork tenderloin into medallions and serve it with the apples, onions, and pan sauce spooned over the top.
Garnish with chopped fresh parsley if desired.

Enjoy your delicious pork tenderloin with apples and onions! It's a perfect meal for a cozy dinner at home.

**Sweet Potato Casserole with Marshmallow Topping**

Ingredients:

For the sweet potato filling:

- 4 large sweet potatoes, peeled and cut into chunks
- 1/4 cup unsalted butter, melted
- 1/4 cup milk (or heavy cream for a richer texture)
- 1/4 cup brown sugar, packed
- 1 teaspoon vanilla extract
- 1/2 teaspoon ground cinnamon
- 1/4 teaspoon ground nutmeg
- 1/4 teaspoon salt

For the marshmallow topping:

- 2 cups mini marshmallows

Instructions:

Preheat your oven to 375°F (190°C). Grease a 9x13 inch baking dish.
Place the sweet potato chunks in a large pot and cover them with water. Bring the water to a boil over high heat, then reduce the heat to medium-low and let the sweet potatoes simmer until they are fork-tender, about 15-20 minutes.
Drain the sweet potatoes and transfer them to a large mixing bowl.
Use a potato masher or fork to mash the sweet potatoes until smooth.
Add the melted butter, milk (or heavy cream), brown sugar, vanilla extract, ground cinnamon, ground nutmeg, and salt to the bowl with the mashed sweet potatoes. Stir until all ingredients are well combined and the mixture is smooth.
Transfer the sweet potato mixture to the prepared baking dish, spreading it out evenly.
Sprinkle the mini marshmallows evenly over the top of the sweet potato mixture, covering it completely.
Place the baking dish in the preheated oven and bake for 15-20 minutes, or until the marshmallows are golden brown and bubbly.
Once done, remove the casserole from the oven and let it cool for a few minutes before serving.
Serve the sweet potato casserole with marshmallow topping warm as a delicious side dish or dessert.

Enjoy the sweet and decadent flavors of this classic sweet potato casserole with marshmallow topping! It's sure to be a hit at your next gathering.

**Creamy Wild Rice Soup**

Ingredients:

- 1 cup wild rice blend
- 6 cups chicken or vegetable broth
- 4 tablespoons unsalted butter
- 1 onion, finely chopped
- 2 carrots, diced
- 2 celery stalks, diced
- 2 cloves garlic, minced
- 1/4 cup all-purpose flour
- 2 cups cooked chicken, shredded (optional)
- 1 cup heavy cream
- Salt and pepper to taste
- Chopped fresh parsley for garnish (optional)

Instructions:

Rinse the wild rice under cold water in a fine-mesh strainer.
In a large pot, bring the chicken or vegetable broth to a boil over high heat. Add the rinsed wild rice to the pot, reduce the heat to low, cover, and let simmer for 45-50 minutes, or until the rice is tender and has absorbed most of the liquid.
In another large pot or Dutch oven, melt the butter over medium heat.
Add the chopped onion, diced carrots, and diced celery to the pot. Cook, stirring occasionally, until the vegetables are softened, about 5-7 minutes.
Add the minced garlic to the pot and cook for another minute, until fragrant.
Sprinkle the flour over the vegetables in the pot and stir to combine, cooking for 1-2 minutes to make a roux.
Gradually pour in the chicken or vegetable broth, stirring constantly to prevent lumps from forming.
Bring the mixture to a simmer and cook, stirring occasionally, until the soup thickens slightly, about 5-7 minutes.
Stir in the cooked chicken (if using) and cooked wild rice into the soup.
Pour in the heavy cream and stir until the soup is heated through.
Season the soup with salt and pepper to taste.
Ladle the creamy wild rice soup into bowls and garnish with chopped fresh parsley if desired.
Serve hot and enjoy the comforting and creamy flavors of this delicious soup!

This creamy wild rice soup is sure to warm you up and satisfy your cravings for a hearty and comforting meal. Feel free to customize it by adding your favorite vegetables or herbs. Enjoy!

**Roast Duck with Orange Sauce**

Ingredients:

For the roast duck:

- 1 whole duck (about 5-6 pounds), giblets removed
- Salt and pepper to taste
- 1 orange, quartered
- 2 sprigs fresh rosemary
- 2 sprigs fresh thyme
- 2 cloves garlic, crushed
- 2 tablespoons olive oil

For the orange sauce:

- 1 cup orange juice
- Zest of 1 orange
- 1/2 cup chicken broth
- 2 tablespoons honey or maple syrup
- 2 tablespoons soy sauce
- 1 tablespoon cornstarch
- 2 tablespoons water
- Salt and pepper to taste

Instructions:

For the roast duck:

> Preheat your oven to 375°F (190°C).
> Pat the duck dry with paper towels, then season the inside and outside of the duck generously with salt and pepper.
> Place the quartered orange, fresh rosemary, fresh thyme, and crushed garlic inside the cavity of the duck.
> Rub the outside of the duck with olive oil, ensuring it's evenly coated.
> Place the duck on a rack in a roasting pan, breast side up.

Roast the duck in the preheated oven for 2-2 1/2 hours, or until the skin is crispy and golden brown and the internal temperature reaches 165°F (74°C) when measured with a meat thermometer inserted into the thickest part of the thigh. Once the duck is done cooking, remove it from the oven and let it rest for 10-15 minutes before carving.

For the orange sauce:

While the duck is roasting, prepare the orange sauce.
In a small saucepan, combine the orange juice, orange zest, chicken broth, honey or maple syrup, and soy sauce. Bring the mixture to a simmer over medium heat.
In a small bowl, mix the cornstarch with water to make a slurry.
Gradually whisk the cornstarch slurry into the saucepan, stirring constantly, until the sauce thickens slightly.
Season the sauce with salt and pepper to taste.
Once the duck has rested, carve it into serving portions and serve with the orange sauce drizzled over the top.
Garnish with additional orange zest or fresh herbs if desired.
Serve hot and enjoy your delicious roast duck with orange sauce!

This roast duck with orange sauce is sure to impress your family and guests with its beautiful presentation and irresistible flavors. It's perfect for special occasions or holiday dinners.

**Cranberry Pecan Stuffing**

Ingredients:

- 8 cups cubed bread (such as French bread or sourdough), preferably stale
- 1/2 cup unsalted butter
- 1 large onion, chopped
- 2 stalks celery, chopped
- 2 cloves garlic, minced
- 1 teaspoon dried sage
- 1 teaspoon dried thyme
- 1/2 teaspoon dried rosemary
- 1/2 teaspoon salt
- 1/4 teaspoon black pepper
- 1 cup chopped pecans, toasted
- 1 cup dried cranberries
- 2-3 cups low-sodium chicken or vegetable broth
- Chopped fresh parsley for garnish (optional)

Instructions:

Preheat your oven to 350°F (175°C). Grease a 9x13 inch baking dish.
Spread the cubed bread out on a baking sheet in a single layer. Toast in the preheated oven for 10-15 minutes, or until the bread is dry and slightly crisp. Alternatively, you can leave the bread cubes out at room temperature for a few hours or overnight to dry out.
In a large skillet, melt the butter over medium heat.
Add the chopped onion and celery to the skillet and cook, stirring occasionally, until the vegetables are softened, about 5-7 minutes.
Stir in the minced garlic, dried sage, dried thyme, dried rosemary, salt, and black pepper. Cook for another minute, until fragrant.
Remove the skillet from the heat and stir in the chopped pecans and dried cranberries.
In a large mixing bowl, combine the toasted bread cubes with the onion, celery, pecan, and cranberry mixture. Toss until well combined.
Gradually pour the chicken or vegetable broth over the bread mixture, stirring gently, until the bread is moistened but not soggy. You may not need to use all of the broth.
Transfer the stuffing mixture to the prepared baking dish, spreading it out evenly.

Cover the baking dish with aluminum foil and bake in the preheated oven for 30 minutes.
Remove the foil and bake for an additional 15-20 minutes, or until the top of the stuffing is golden brown and crispy.
Remove the stuffing from the oven and let it cool for a few minutes before serving.
Garnish with chopped fresh parsley if desired, and serve hot as a delicious side dish.

Enjoy your flavorful and festive cranberry pecan stuffing! It's perfect for Thanksgiving, Christmas, or any holiday feast.

**Baked Brie with Cranberry Compote**

Ingredients:

For the cranberry compote:

- 1 cup fresh or frozen cranberries
- 1/4 cup granulated sugar
- 1/4 cup water
- Zest and juice of 1 orange
- 1 cinnamon stick (optional)

For the baked brie:

- 1 round of brie cheese (about 8-10 ounces)
- 1 sheet of puff pastry, thawed according to package instructions
- 1 egg, beaten (for egg wash)
- 1 tablespoon honey (optional)
- Fresh rosemary sprigs for garnish (optional)
- Crackers or sliced baguette, for serving

Instructions:

For the cranberry compote:

In a small saucepan, combine the cranberries, granulated sugar, water, orange zest, orange juice, and cinnamon stick (if using).
Bring the mixture to a boil over medium-high heat, then reduce the heat to low and let it simmer for 10-15 minutes, stirring occasionally, until the cranberries burst and the mixture thickens into a compote-like consistency.
Remove the cinnamon stick from the compote and let it cool slightly before serving. You can also refrigerate the compote until ready to use.

For the baked brie:

Preheat your oven to 375°F (190°C). Line a baking sheet with parchment paper. Roll out the thawed puff pastry sheet on a lightly floured surface into a large square or rectangle, depending on the size of your brie round.

Place the brie round in the center of the puff pastry. If desired, you can trim any excess puff pastry around the brie.

Spoon the cranberry compote over the top of the brie.

Fold the edges of the puff pastry up and over the brie, covering it completely. Pinch the seams together to seal the pastry.

Brush the beaten egg over the surface of the puff pastry for a golden finish.

Place the wrapped brie on the prepared baking sheet and bake in the preheated oven for 20-25 minutes, or until the pastry is golden brown and puffed up.

Remove the baked brie from the oven and let it cool for a few minutes before serving.

Drizzle the baked brie with honey (if using) and garnish with fresh rosemary sprigs for a festive touch.

Serve the baked brie warm with crackers or sliced baguette, along with any remaining cranberry compote on the side.

Enjoy the creamy, melty brie paired with the sweet and tangy cranberry compote—it's a delightful appetizer that's sure to impress your guests!

**Beef Wellington**

Ingredients:

- 1 1/2 to 2 pounds beef tenderloin, trimmed
- Salt and pepper to taste
- 2 tablespoons olive oil
- 2 tablespoons Dijon mustard
- 8 ounces cremini mushrooms, finely chopped
- 2 cloves garlic, minced
- 2 tablespoons butter
- 1 tablespoon fresh thyme leaves
- 1/4 cup dry white wine (optional)
- 1 sheet puff pastry, thawed if frozen
- 1 egg, beaten (for egg wash)
- Salt flakes or coarse sea salt, for garnish (optional)

Instructions:

Preheat your oven to 425°F (220°C).
Season the beef tenderloin generously with salt and pepper.
Heat the olive oil in a large skillet over high heat. Sear the beef tenderloin on all sides until browned, about 2 minutes per side. Remove the beef from the skillet and let it cool slightly.
Brush the cooled beef tenderloin with Dijon mustard on all sides. Set aside.
In the same skillet, melt the butter over medium heat. Add the finely chopped mushrooms, minced garlic, and fresh thyme leaves. Cook, stirring occasionally, until the mushrooms release their moisture and turn golden brown, about 5-7 minutes.
If using, pour in the dry white wine to deglaze the skillet, scraping up any browned bits from the bottom. Cook until the wine has evaporated. Remove the mushroom mixture from the heat and let it cool slightly.
Roll out the puff pastry sheet on a lightly floured surface into a rectangle large enough to wrap around the beef tenderloin.
Spread the cooled mushroom mixture evenly over the puff pastry sheet.
Place the seared beef tenderloin on top of the mushroom mixture.
Carefully wrap the puff pastry around the beef tenderloin, pressing the edges to seal and trimming any excess pastry if necessary. Pinch the seams together to seal tightly.

Place the wrapped beef Wellington seam side down on a baking sheet lined with parchment paper.
Brush the beaten egg over the surface of the puff pastry for a golden finish.
Using a sharp knife, score the top of the puff pastry lightly in a crisscross pattern. Be careful not to cut through the pastry.
Optional: Sprinkle salt flakes or coarse sea salt over the top of the puff pastry for added flavor and texture.
Bake the beef Wellington in the preheated oven for 35-40 minutes, or until the pastry is golden brown and crisp, and the beef reaches your desired level of doneness. For medium-rare, aim for an internal temperature of 130-135°F (54-57°C) when measured with a meat thermometer inserted into the center of the beef.
Once done, remove the beef Wellington from the oven and let it rest for 10 minutes before slicing.
Slice the beef Wellington into thick portions and serve immediately.

Enjoy the decadent and flavorful beef Wellington as a stunning centerpiece for your holiday table or special occasion meal!

**Creamy Cauliflower Gratin**

Ingredients:

- 1 large head cauliflower, cut into florets
- 2 tablespoons unsalted butter
- 2 tablespoons all-purpose flour
- 2 cups milk
- 1/2 cup heavy cream
- 2 cloves garlic, minced
- 1 teaspoon Dijon mustard
- 1/2 teaspoon dried thyme
- Salt and pepper to taste
- 1 cup shredded Gruyère cheese (or your preferred cheese)
- 1/4 cup grated Parmesan cheese
- 1/4 cup breadcrumbs
- Chopped fresh parsley for garnish (optional)

Instructions:

Preheat your oven to 375°F (190°C). Grease a baking dish with butter or cooking spray.

Bring a large pot of salted water to a boil. Add the cauliflower florets and cook for 5-6 minutes, or until slightly tender. Drain the cauliflower and set aside.

In a saucepan, melt the butter over medium heat. Add the minced garlic and cook for 1-2 minutes, until fragrant.

Stir in the flour and cook for 1-2 minutes, stirring constantly, to make a roux.

Gradually whisk in the milk and heavy cream, stirring constantly to prevent lumps from forming.

Cook the sauce until it thickens, about 5-7 minutes, stirring frequently.

Stir in the Dijon mustard, dried thyme, salt, and pepper to taste.

Remove the saucepan from the heat and stir in the shredded Gruyère cheese until melted and smooth.

Place the cooked cauliflower florets in the prepared baking dish.

Pour the cheese sauce over the cauliflower, ensuring it's evenly coated.

In a small bowl, combine the grated Parmesan cheese and breadcrumbs.

Sprinkle the mixture evenly over the top of the cauliflower.

Bake the cauliflower gratin in the preheated oven for 25-30 minutes, or until the top is golden brown and bubbly.

Once done, remove the cauliflower gratin from the oven and let it cool for a few minutes before serving.
Garnish with chopped fresh parsley if desired, and serve hot as a delicious side dish.

Enjoy the creamy and cheesy goodness of this cauliflower gratin—it's sure to be a hit with your family and friends!

**Pear and Gorgonzola Salad**

Ingredients:

- 4 cups mixed salad greens (such as baby spinach, arugula, and/or mixed greens)
- 2 ripe pears, thinly sliced
- 1/2 cup crumbled Gorgonzola cheese (or blue cheese)
- 1/4 cup chopped walnuts or pecans, toasted
- 2 tablespoons balsamic vinegar
- 2 tablespoons extra virgin olive oil
- 1 tablespoon honey
- Salt and pepper to taste

Instructions:

In a large salad bowl, combine the mixed salad greens, thinly sliced pears, crumbled Gorgonzola cheese, and toasted walnuts or pecans.
In a small bowl or jar, whisk together the balsamic vinegar, extra virgin olive oil, honey, salt, and pepper to make the dressing.
Drizzle the dressing over the salad ingredients in the bowl.
Gently toss the salad until everything is evenly coated with the dressing.
Taste and adjust seasoning with salt and pepper if needed.
Serve the pear and Gorgonzola salad immediately as a refreshing appetizer or side dish.

Enjoy the delightful combination of flavors and textures in this pear and Gorgonzola salad—it's sure to be a hit at your next meal! You can also customize the salad by adding other ingredients like dried cranberries, sliced red onions, or avocado slices, if desired.

**Chicken Pot Pie**

Ingredients:

For the filling:

- 2 tablespoons unsalted butter
- 1 onion, diced
- 2 carrots, diced
- 2 celery stalks, diced
- 2 cloves garlic, minced
- 1/4 cup all-purpose flour
- 2 cups chicken broth
- 1 cup milk
- 2 cups cooked chicken, diced or shredded
- 1 cup frozen peas
- 1 teaspoon dried thyme
- Salt and pepper to taste

For the pastry crust:

- 1 1/2 cups all-purpose flour
- 1/2 teaspoon salt
- 1/2 cup unsalted butter, cold and cubed
- 4-6 tablespoons ice water

Instructions:

For the filling:

Preheat your oven to 400°F (200°C).
In a large skillet or saucepan, melt the butter over medium heat.
Add the diced onion, carrots, and celery to the skillet. Cook, stirring occasionally, until the vegetables are softened, about 5-7 minutes.
Stir in the minced garlic and cook for another minute, until fragrant.
Sprinkle the flour over the vegetables in the skillet and stir to combine, cooking for 1-2 minutes to make a roux.
Gradually pour in the chicken broth and milk, stirring constantly, until the mixture is smooth.

Bring the mixture to a simmer and cook, stirring occasionally, until it thickens, about 5-7 minutes.

Stir in the cooked chicken, frozen peas, dried thyme, salt, and pepper. Cook for another 2-3 minutes, until the filling is heated through and the peas are tender. Remove the skillet from the heat.

For the pastry crust:

In a large mixing bowl, combine the flour and salt.

Add the cold, cubed butter to the flour mixture. Using a pastry cutter or your fingers, cut the butter into the flour until the mixture resembles coarse crumbs.

Gradually add the ice water, 1 tablespoon at a time, stirring gently, until the dough comes together. Be careful not to overwork the dough.

Shape the dough into a disk, wrap it in plastic wrap, and refrigerate it for at least 30 minutes.

Assembling the pot pie:

Transfer the chicken and vegetable filling to a 9-inch pie dish or a casserole dish.

On a lightly floured surface, roll out the chilled pastry dough into a circle large enough to cover the pie dish.

Carefully place the pastry dough over the filling in the pie dish. Trim any excess dough and crimp the edges to seal.

Use a sharp knife to make a few slits in the pastry crust to allow steam to escape during baking.

Optional: Brush the pastry crust with a beaten egg for a golden finish.

Place the pot pie in the preheated oven and bake for 30-35 minutes, or until the pastry crust is golden brown and the filling is bubbling.

Once done, remove the pot pie from the oven and let it cool for a few minutes before serving.

Enjoy the comforting and delicious flavors of homemade chicken pot pie! Serve it hot as a satisfying meal for any occasion.

**Buttermilk Biscuits**

Ingredients:

- 2 cups all-purpose flour, plus more for dusting
- 1 tablespoon baking powder
- 1 teaspoon sugar
- 1/2 teaspoon salt
- 1/2 cup (1 stick) unsalted butter, cold and cut into small cubes
- 3/4 cup buttermilk, cold

Instructions:

Preheat your oven to 425°F (220°C). Line a baking sheet with parchment paper or lightly grease it with butter.
In a large mixing bowl, whisk together the all-purpose flour, baking powder, sugar, and salt until well combined.
Add the cold, cubed butter to the flour mixture. Using a pastry cutter or your fingertips, cut the butter into the flour until the mixture resembles coarse crumbs with some pea-sized pieces of butter remaining.
Make a well in the center of the flour mixture and pour in the cold buttermilk.
Use a fork or spatula to gently stir the mixture until it just comes together into a shaggy dough. Be careful not to overmix.
Turn the dough out onto a lightly floured surface. Use your hands to gently pat the dough into a rectangle or circle, about 1/2 to 3/4 inch thick.
Fold the dough in half and pat it out again. Repeat this process 2-3 more times, being careful not to overwork the dough. This will help create layers in the biscuits.
Use a biscuit cutter or round cookie cutter to cut out biscuits from the dough. Press straight down without twisting to cut out the biscuits, as twisting can seal the edges and prevent them from rising properly.
Place the cut biscuits onto the prepared baking sheet, spacing them about 1 inch apart.
Gather any remaining dough scraps and gently pat them together to cut out more biscuits.
Once all the biscuits are cut out, bake them in the preheated oven for 12-15 minutes, or until they are golden brown on top and cooked through.
Remove the biscuits from the oven and let them cool for a few minutes before serving.

Enjoy the warm, buttery goodness of homemade buttermilk biscuits! Serve them with butter, jam, honey, gravy, or your favorite toppings for a delicious treat.

**Roasted Garlic Mashed Cauliflower**

Ingredients:

- 1 head of cauliflower, cut into florets
- 4 cloves garlic, peeled
- 2 tablespoons olive oil
- Salt and pepper to taste
- 2 tablespoons unsalted butter
- 1/4 cup grated Parmesan cheese
- 1/4 cup heavy cream (or milk for a lighter option)
- Chopped fresh chives or parsley for garnish (optional)

Instructions:

Preheat your oven to 400°F (200°C).
Place the cauliflower florets and peeled garlic cloves on a baking sheet. Drizzle with olive oil and season with salt and pepper to taste. Toss to coat evenly.
Roast the cauliflower and garlic in the preheated oven for 25-30 minutes, or until the cauliflower is tender and golden brown, and the garlic is soft and caramelized.
Remove the roasted cauliflower and garlic from the oven and let them cool slightly.
Transfer the roasted cauliflower and garlic to a food processor or blender. Add the butter, grated Parmesan cheese, and heavy cream (or milk).
Blend the mixture until smooth and creamy. You may need to stop and scrape down the sides of the bowl occasionally to ensure everything is evenly blended.
Taste the mashed cauliflower and adjust seasoning with salt and pepper if needed.
Once the desired consistency and flavor are achieved, transfer the mashed cauliflower to a serving dish.
Garnish with chopped fresh chives or parsley if desired.
Serve the roasted garlic mashed cauliflower hot as a delicious and healthy side dish.

Enjoy the creamy and flavorful goodness of roasted garlic mashed cauliflower! It's a perfect accompaniment to any meal and a great way to add more vegetables to your diet.

**Maple Glazed Salmon**

Ingredients:

- 4 salmon fillets, skin-on or skinless
- Salt and pepper to taste
- 1/4 cup maple syrup
- 2 tablespoons soy sauce or tamari (for gluten-free option)
- 1 tablespoon Dijon mustard
- 1 tablespoon olive oil
- 2 cloves garlic, minced
- 1 tablespoon fresh lemon juice
- Optional: Sesame seeds, chopped green onions, or chopped parsley for garnish

Instructions:

Preheat your oven to 400°F (200°C). Line a baking sheet with parchment paper or lightly grease it with olive oil.

Season the salmon fillets with salt and pepper on both sides.

In a small bowl, whisk together the maple syrup, soy sauce or tamari, Dijon mustard, olive oil, minced garlic, and fresh lemon juice until well combined.

Place the seasoned salmon fillets on the prepared baking sheet.

Brush the maple glaze mixture generously over the top of each salmon fillet, coating them evenly.

Optional: Sprinkle sesame seeds over the glazed salmon for added flavor and texture.

Place the baking sheet in the preheated oven and bake the salmon for 12-15 minutes, or until the salmon is cooked through and flakes easily with a fork.

Once done, remove the salmon from the oven and let it rest for a few minutes before serving.

Garnish the maple glazed salmon with chopped green onions or parsley if desired.

Serve the salmon hot with your favorite side dishes, such as roasted vegetables, rice, or salad.

Enjoy the delicious combination of sweet and savory flavors in this maple glazed salmon dish! It's quick and easy to make, making it perfect for a weeknight dinner or special occasion meal.

**Vegetarian Shepherd's Pie**

Ingredients:

For the mashed potato topping:

- 2 pounds potatoes (such as russet or Yukon gold), peeled and cut into chunks
- 4 tablespoons unsalted butter
- 1/2 cup milk (or vegetable broth for a dairy-free option)
- Salt and pepper to taste

For the vegetable filling:

- 2 tablespoons olive oil
- 1 onion, chopped
- 2 carrots, diced
- 2 celery stalks, diced
- 2 cloves garlic, minced
- 1 bell pepper, diced
- 1 cup mushrooms, diced
- 1 cup frozen peas
- 1 cup corn kernels (fresh, canned, or frozen)
- 1 teaspoon dried thyme
- 1 teaspoon dried rosemary
- 2 tablespoons all-purpose flour
- 1 cup vegetable broth
- 2 tablespoons tomato paste
- Salt and pepper to taste

Instructions:

For the mashed potato topping:

> Place the peeled and chopped potatoes in a large pot of salted water. Bring the water to a boil over high heat, then reduce the heat to medium-low and let the potatoes simmer until they are fork-tender, about 15-20 minutes.
> Drain the cooked potatoes and return them to the pot.
> Add the butter and milk (or vegetable broth) to the pot with the potatoes. Use a potato masher or fork to mash the potatoes until smooth and creamy. Season with salt and pepper to taste. Set aside.

For the vegetable filling:

- Preheat your oven to 375°F (190°C).
- In a large skillet or saucepan, heat the olive oil over medium heat.
- Add the chopped onion, diced carrots, diced celery, and minced garlic to the skillet. Cook, stirring occasionally, until the vegetables are softened, about 5-7 minutes.
- Add the diced bell pepper and mushrooms to the skillet. Cook for another 3-4 minutes, until the mushrooms release their moisture and start to brown.
- Stir in the frozen peas and corn kernels, dried thyme, and dried rosemary. Cook for 2-3 minutes, until the vegetables are heated through.
- Sprinkle the flour over the vegetable mixture in the skillet and stir to coat the vegetables evenly.
- Gradually pour in the vegetable broth, stirring constantly, until the mixture thickens into a gravy-like consistency.
- Stir in the tomato paste until well combined. Season the vegetable filling with salt and pepper to taste.

Assembling the vegetarian shepherd's pie:

- Transfer the vegetable filling to a 9x13 inch baking dish or a similar-sized casserole dish, spreading it out evenly.
- Spoon the mashed potato topping over the vegetable filling, spreading it out with a spatula to cover the filling completely.
- Use a fork to create texture on the surface of the mashed potatoes, if desired.
- Place the baking dish in the preheated oven and bake the shepherd's pie for 25-30 minutes, or until the mashed potatoes are golden brown and the filling is bubbly around the edges.
- Once done, remove the shepherd's pie from the oven and let it cool for a few minutes before serving.
- Serve the vegetarian shepherd's pie hot as a delicious and satisfying meal.

Enjoy the comforting and flavorful goodness of this vegetarian shepherd's pie—it's sure to be a hit with your family and friends!

**Mulled Wine**

Ingredients:

- 1 bottle (750 ml) red wine (such as Cabernet Sauvignon, Merlot, or Zinfandel)
- 1/4 cup honey or maple syrup (adjust to taste)
- 1 orange, sliced
- 1 lemon, sliced
- 6 whole cloves
- 2 cinnamon sticks
- 2 star anise
- 1/4 teaspoon ground nutmeg
- Optional garnishes: additional orange or lemon slices, cinnamon sticks, star anise

Instructions:

Pour the red wine into a large saucepan or pot.
Add the honey or maple syrup, orange slices, lemon slices, whole cloves, cinnamon sticks, star anise, and ground nutmeg to the pot.
Stir the mixture to combine.
Place the pot over medium heat and slowly bring the wine mixture to a simmer. Do not boil, as boiling can cause the alcohol to evaporate.
Once the wine is simmering, reduce the heat to low and let it continue to simmer for 15-20 minutes, stirring occasionally to allow the flavors to meld together.
Taste the mulled wine and adjust the sweetness or spices to your liking. You can add more honey or maple syrup for sweetness, or more cloves, cinnamon, or nutmeg for spiciness.
Once the mulled wine is ready, remove it from the heat and strain out the spices and citrus slices.
Ladle the mulled wine into mugs or glasses.
Optional: Garnish each serving with additional orange or lemon slices, cinnamon sticks, or star anise for a festive touch.
Serve the mulled wine hot and enjoy its warm and fragrant flavors!

Mulled wine is perfect for holiday gatherings, cozy nights by the fire, or any occasion where you want to add a touch of warmth and cheer to your celebration. Cheers!

**Roasted Chestnuts**

Ingredients:

- Fresh chestnuts (as many as you'd like to roast)

Instructions:

Preheat your oven to 425°F (220°C).
Using a sharp knife, carefully score an "X" onto the flat side of each chestnut. This allows steam to escape during roasting and prevents the chestnuts from exploding.
Place the scored chestnuts on a baking sheet in a single layer, with the scored side facing up.
Roast the chestnuts in the preheated oven for 20-25 minutes, or until the shells have split open and the insides are tender and cooked through.
Remove the roasted chestnuts from the oven and let them cool slightly before handling, as they will be very hot.
Once the chestnuts are cool enough to handle, peel away the outer shell and the thin inner skin to reveal the creamy, nutty flesh inside.
Enjoy the roasted chestnuts warm as a tasty snack or use them in your favorite recipes.

Roasted chestnuts are delicious on their own, but you can also add them to stuffing, salads, or desserts for a unique and flavorful touch. Enjoy!

**Winter Citrus Salad**

Ingredients:

- 4 cups mixed salad greens (such as arugula, spinach, or mixed greens)
- 2 oranges (such as navel oranges or blood oranges), peeled and sliced into rounds or segments
- 2 grapefruits (such as pink or red grapefruits), peeled and sliced into rounds or segments
- 1 large avocado, peeled, pitted, and sliced
- 1/4 cup red onion, thinly sliced
- 1/4 cup toasted nuts or seeds (such as almonds, walnuts, or pumpkin seeds)
- Optional: Crumbled feta or goat cheese for garnish

For the dressing:

- 3 tablespoons extra virgin olive oil
- 2 tablespoons fresh lemon juice
- 1 tablespoon honey or maple syrup
- Salt and pepper to taste

Instructions:

In a small bowl, whisk together the extra virgin olive oil, fresh lemon juice, honey or maple syrup, salt, and pepper to make the dressing. Set aside.
Arrange the mixed salad greens on a serving platter or in a large salad bowl.
Arrange the orange and grapefruit slices or segments on top of the salad greens.
Add the sliced avocado and thinly sliced red onion on top of the citrus slices.
Drizzle the dressing over the salad, tossing gently to coat the ingredients evenly.
Sprinkle the toasted nuts or seeds over the salad.
Optional: Garnish the salad with crumbled feta or goat cheese for an extra burst of flavor.
Serve the winter citrus salad immediately as a refreshing appetizer or side dish.

This winter citrus salad is bursting with bright and tangy flavors, making it a perfect complement to any meal. Enjoy its refreshing taste and vibrant colors during the colder months!

**Beef Bourguignon**

Ingredients:

- 2 pounds beef chuck roast, cut into 1-inch cubes
- Salt and pepper to taste
- 2 tablespoons olive oil
- 4 slices bacon, chopped
- 1 onion, chopped
- 2 carrots, peeled and chopped
- 2 cloves garlic, minced
- 2 tablespoons all-purpose flour
- 1 cup red wine (such as Pinot Noir or Burgundy)
- 2 cups beef broth
- 2 tablespoons tomato paste
- 1 teaspoon dried thyme
- 2 bay leaves
- 1 pound small potatoes, halved
- 1/2 pound mushrooms, quartered
- Chopped fresh parsley for garnish

Instructions:

Preheat your oven to 325°F (160°C).
Season the beef cubes with salt and pepper to taste.
Heat the olive oil in a large Dutch oven or oven-safe pot over medium-high heat.
Add the seasoned beef cubes to the pot in batches, making sure not to overcrowd the pan. Brown the beef cubes on all sides, about 3-4 minutes per batch. Remove the browned beef cubes from the pot and set aside.
In the same pot, add the chopped bacon and cook until crispy. Remove the crispy bacon from the pot and set aside with the beef cubes.
Add the chopped onion and carrots to the pot. Cook, stirring occasionally, until the vegetables are softened, about 5-7 minutes.
Add the minced garlic and cook for another minute, until fragrant.
Sprinkle the flour over the vegetables in the pot and stir to coat evenly.
Pour in the red wine, scraping up any browned bits from the bottom of the pot.
Bring the mixture to a simmer and cook for 2-3 minutes, until slightly reduced.
Stir in the beef broth, tomato paste, dried thyme, and bay leaves. Return the browned beef cubes and crispy bacon to the pot. Bring the mixture to a simmer.

Cover the pot with a lid and transfer it to the preheated oven. Let the beef bourguignon cook in the oven for 2 hours, stirring occasionally.

After 2 hours, remove the pot from the oven and add the halved potatoes and quartered mushrooms to the stew. Stir to combine.

Return the pot to the oven and continue cooking for another 45 minutes to 1 hour, or until the beef is tender and the potatoes are cooked through.

Once done, remove the pot from the oven and discard the bay leaves.

Taste the beef bourguignon and adjust seasoning with salt and pepper if needed.

Garnish the beef bourguignon with chopped fresh parsley before serving.

Enjoy the rich and comforting flavors of beef bourguignon served hot with crusty bread or over mashed potatoes. It's a delicious and satisfying meal that's perfect for special occasions or cozy dinners at home.

**Pumpkin Cheesecake**

Ingredients:

For the crust:

- 1 1/2 cups graham cracker crumbs
- 1/4 cup granulated sugar
- 1/2 cup unsalted butter, melted

For the cheesecake filling:

- 3 (8-ounce) packages cream cheese, softened
- 1 cup granulated sugar
- 1 teaspoon vanilla extract
- 3 large eggs
- 1 cup pumpkin puree (canned or homemade)
- 1 teaspoon ground cinnamon
- 1/2 teaspoon ground nutmeg
- 1/4 teaspoon ground ginger
- 1/4 teaspoon ground cloves

For the topping:

- 1 cup whipped cream
- Ground cinnamon or nutmeg for garnish (optional)

Instructions:

For the crust:

Preheat your oven to 325°F (160°C). Grease a 9-inch springform pan with butter or non-stick cooking spray.
In a mixing bowl, combine the graham cracker crumbs, granulated sugar, and melted butter. Stir until the mixture resembles coarse crumbs and is well combined.
Press the crumb mixture firmly and evenly into the bottom of the prepared springform pan, using the back of a spoon or your fingers.
Bake the crust in the preheated oven for 10 minutes. Remove from the oven and let it cool while you prepare the cheesecake filling.

For the cheesecake filling:

In a large mixing bowl, beat the softened cream cheese, granulated sugar, and vanilla extract until smooth and creamy, using an electric mixer on medium speed.
Add the eggs one at a time, beating well after each addition, until fully incorporated.
Add the pumpkin puree, ground cinnamon, ground nutmeg, ground ginger, and ground cloves to the cream cheese mixture. Beat until smooth and well combined.

Assembling and baking the cheesecake:

Pour the pumpkin cheesecake filling over the cooled crust in the springform pan, spreading it out evenly with a spatula.
Tap the pan gently on the counter to release any air bubbles in the cheesecake filling.
Place the springform pan in a large roasting pan or baking dish. Fill the roasting pan or baking dish with hot water to create a water bath for the cheesecake. The water should come about halfway up the sides of the springform pan.
Carefully transfer the roasting pan or baking dish with the cheesecake to the preheated oven.
Bake the cheesecake in the water bath for 60-70 minutes, or until the edges are set and the center is slightly jiggly.
Turn off the oven and leave the cheesecake inside with the oven door slightly ajar for about 1 hour to cool gradually.
Remove the cheesecake from the oven and refrigerate it for at least 4 hours or overnight to chill and set.

For the topping:

Just before serving, spread whipped cream over the top of the chilled cheesecake.
Optional: Sprinkle ground cinnamon or nutmeg over the whipped cream for garnish.
Slice the pumpkin cheesecake and serve chilled.

Enjoy the creamy and flavorful indulgence of pumpkin cheesecake—it's a perfect dessert for fall celebrations, Thanksgiving, or any occasion where you want to impress your guests with a delicious treat!

**Cornbread Stuffing**

Ingredients:

- 8 cups cornbread, cut into cubes and dried overnight (store-bought or homemade)
- 4 tablespoons unsalted butter
- 1 onion, diced
- 2 stalks celery, diced
- 2 cloves garlic, minced
- 1 teaspoon dried sage
- 1 teaspoon dried thyme
- 1/2 teaspoon dried rosemary
- Salt and pepper to taste
- 2 cups vegetable or chicken broth, plus more if needed
- 2 eggs, beaten

Instructions:

Preheat your oven to 350°F (175°C). Grease a 9x13 inch baking dish with butter or non-stick cooking spray.
In a large skillet, melt the butter over medium heat.
Add the diced onion and celery to the skillet. Cook, stirring occasionally, until the vegetables are softened, about 5-7 minutes.
Add the minced garlic, dried sage, dried thyme, and dried rosemary to the skillet. Cook for another minute, until fragrant. Season with salt and pepper to taste.
In a large mixing bowl, combine the dried cornbread cubes with the cooked vegetable mixture.
Pour the vegetable or chicken broth over the cornbread mixture, starting with 1 1/2 cups and adding more as needed to moisten the mixture. The cornbread should be moist but not soggy.
Add the beaten eggs to the cornbread mixture and stir until everything is well combined.
Transfer the cornbread stuffing mixture to the prepared baking dish, spreading it out evenly.
Cover the baking dish with aluminum foil and bake in the preheated oven for 30 minutes.
After 30 minutes, remove the foil and continue baking for another 15-20 minutes, or until the top is golden brown and crispy.

Once done, remove the cornbread stuffing from the oven and let it cool for a few minutes before serving.
Serve the cornbread stuffing hot as a delicious and comforting side dish for your Thanksgiving or holiday meal.

Enjoy the savory flavors and crispy texture of this classic cornbread stuffing—it's sure to be a hit with your family and friends! You can also customize the recipe by adding chopped herbs, dried fruit, nuts, or sausage for extra flavor and texture.

**Herb Crusted Rack of Lamb**

Ingredients:

- 1 rack of lamb, frenched (about 1 1/2 to 2 pounds)
- Salt and pepper to taste
- 2 tablespoons Dijon mustard
- 2 cloves garlic, minced
- 2 tablespoons chopped fresh herbs (such as rosemary, thyme, and parsley)
- 1/2 cup breadcrumbs
- 2 tablespoons olive oil

Instructions:

Preheat your oven to 400°F (200°C).
Season the rack of lamb generously with salt and pepper on all sides.
In a small bowl, mix together the Dijon mustard, minced garlic, and chopped fresh herbs.
Spread the herb and mustard mixture evenly over the surface of the rack of lamb.
In another bowl, combine the breadcrumbs and olive oil to make the herb crust.
Press the breadcrumb mixture onto the herb-coated surface of the rack of lamb, covering it evenly.
Place the rack of lamb on a roasting pan or baking sheet, bone side down.
Roast the rack of lamb in the preheated oven for 20-25 minutes for medium-rare, or until the internal temperature reaches 125-130°F (52-54°C) on a meat thermometer.
If you prefer your lamb cooked to a different level of doneness, adjust the cooking time accordingly:
- For rare: 15-20 minutes, with an internal temperature of 120-125°F (49-52°C)
- For medium: 25-30 minutes, with an internal temperature of 130-135°F (54-57°C)
- For well-done: 35-40 minutes, with an internal temperature of 140°F (60°C) or higher

Once done, remove the rack of lamb from the oven and let it rest for 5-10 minutes before slicing.
To serve, slice the rack of lamb between the bones into individual chops.
Serve the herb-crusted rack of lamb hot as a delicious and impressive main course.

Enjoy the succulent and flavorful herb-crusted rack of lamb—it's sure to impress your guests and elevate any meal! Pair it with roasted vegetables, mashed potatoes, or a simple salad for a complete and satisfying dining experience.

**Glazed Sweet Potatoes**

Ingredients:

- 3-4 medium sweet potatoes, peeled and sliced into rounds or cubes
- 2 tablespoons unsalted butter
- 1/4 cup brown sugar (adjust to taste)
- 1/4 cup maple syrup or honey
- 1 teaspoon ground cinnamon
- 1/4 teaspoon ground nutmeg
- Salt to taste
- Chopped fresh parsley or pecans for garnish (optional)

Instructions:

Preheat your oven to 375°F (190°C).
Place the sliced sweet potatoes in a large mixing bowl.
In a small saucepan, melt the butter over medium heat.
Add the brown sugar, maple syrup or honey, ground cinnamon, ground nutmeg, and a pinch of salt to the melted butter. Stir until the sugar is dissolved and the mixture is smooth and well combined.
Pour the glaze mixture over the sliced sweet potatoes in the mixing bowl. Toss until the sweet potatoes are evenly coated with the glaze.
Arrange the glazed sweet potatoes in a single layer in a baking dish or on a baking sheet lined with parchment paper.
Cover the baking dish with aluminum foil and bake in the preheated oven for 25-30 minutes, or until the sweet potatoes are tender when pierced with a fork.
Remove the aluminum foil and continue baking for an additional 10-15 minutes, or until the sweet potatoes are caramelized and glazed.
Once done, remove the glazed sweet potatoes from the oven and let them cool for a few minutes.
Optional: Garnish the glazed sweet potatoes with chopped fresh parsley or pecans for added flavor and texture.
Serve the glazed sweet potatoes hot as a delicious and comforting side dish.

Enjoy the sweet and savory flavors of these glazed sweet potatoes—they're sure to be a hit at your next meal! They're perfect for Thanksgiving, Christmas, or any occasion where you want to add a touch of sweetness to your dinner table.

**Mushroom Wellington**

Ingredients:

- 1 sheet of puff pastry (store-bought or homemade)
- 2 tablespoons olive oil
- 1 onion, finely chopped
- 2 cloves garlic, minced
- 1 pound (450g) mushrooms, finely chopped (such as button mushrooms, cremini, or portobello)
- 1 teaspoon dried thyme
- 1 teaspoon dried rosemary
- Salt and pepper to taste
- 1/4 cup dry white wine (optional)
- 1/4 cup breadcrumbs (optional, for absorbing excess moisture)
- 1/2 cup chopped fresh parsley
- 1/2 cup chopped walnuts or pecans (optional, for added texture)
- 1/2 cup vegan cream cheese or cashew cream (optional, for added creaminess)
- 1/4 cup Dijon mustard
- 1 tablespoon soy sauce or tamari (for vegan option)
- Flour, for dusting
- Vegan egg wash (1 tablespoon plant-based milk mixed with 1 teaspoon maple syrup or agave syrup)

Instructions:

Preheat your oven to 400°F (200°C).

Heat the olive oil in a large skillet over medium heat. Add the chopped onion and garlic, and sauté until softened and fragrant, about 3-4 minutes.

Add the chopped mushrooms to the skillet and cook, stirring occasionally, until the mushrooms release their moisture and begin to brown, about 8-10 minutes.

Stir in the dried thyme, dried rosemary, salt, and pepper. If using, add the white wine to deglaze the pan, scraping up any browned bits from the bottom. Cook until the wine has evaporated.

If there is excess moisture in the skillet, stir in the breadcrumbs to absorb it. This will prevent the puff pastry from becoming soggy.

Remove the skillet from the heat and stir in the chopped parsley, chopped nuts (if using), and vegan cream cheese or cashew cream (if using). Let the mixture cool slightly.

Roll out the puff pastry on a lightly floured surface into a rectangle large enough to encase the mushroom filling. Spread the Dijon mustard evenly over the puff pastry.

Spoon the mushroom mixture onto one half of the puff pastry, leaving a border around the edges. Drizzle the soy sauce or tamari over the mushroom filling.

Fold the other half of the puff pastry over the filling to encase it completely. Press the edges together to seal, and crimp with a fork or your fingers to create a decorative edge.

Transfer the Mushroom Wellington to a baking sheet lined with parchment paper. Brush the top with the vegan egg wash for a golden finish.

Using a sharp knife, make a few small slits in the top of the pastry to allow steam to escape during baking.

Bake the Mushroom Wellington in the preheated oven for 25-30 minutes, or until the pastry is golden brown and puffed up.

Remove from the oven and let it cool for a few minutes before slicing and serving.

Serve the Mushroom Wellington hot, garnished with additional chopped parsley if desired.

Enjoy the savory and flavorful Mushroom Wellington as a delicious main course for a special dinner or holiday celebration!

**Cranberry Orange Bread**

Ingredients:

- 2 cups all-purpose flour
- 1 cup granulated sugar
- 1 1/2 teaspoons baking powder
- 1/2 teaspoon baking soda
- 1/2 teaspoon salt
- 1 cup fresh or frozen cranberries, coarsely chopped
- Zest of 1 orange
- 3/4 cup freshly squeezed orange juice (from about 2-3 oranges)
- 1/4 cup vegetable oil or melted butter
- 1 large egg
- 1 teaspoon vanilla extract

For the optional glaze:

- 1 cup powdered sugar
- 2-3 tablespoons freshly squeezed orange juice

Instructions:

Preheat your oven to 350°F (175°C). Grease a 9x5-inch loaf pan or line it with parchment paper.
In a large mixing bowl, whisk together the flour, sugar, baking powder, baking soda, and salt until well combined.
Stir in the chopped cranberries and orange zest until evenly distributed throughout the dry ingredients.
In a separate bowl, whisk together the freshly squeezed orange juice, vegetable oil or melted butter, egg, and vanilla extract until well combined.
Pour the wet ingredients into the dry ingredients and stir until just combined. Do not overmix; a few lumps are okay.
Pour the batter into the prepared loaf pan and spread it out evenly.
Bake in the preheated oven for 50-60 minutes, or until a toothpick inserted into the center of the bread comes out clean.
Remove the bread from the oven and let it cool in the pan for 10-15 minutes before transferring it to a wire rack to cool completely.

If desired, prepare the optional glaze by whisking together the powdered sugar and freshly squeezed orange juice in a small bowl until smooth. Drizzle the glaze over the cooled bread.
Let the glaze set for a few minutes before slicing the bread.
Slice the cranberry orange bread and serve it at room temperature.
Enjoy the delicious combination of tart cranberries and citrusy orange flavors in this delightful bread!

This cranberry orange bread is perfect for breakfast, brunch, or as a snack any time of the day. It's moist, flavorful, and bursting with seasonal flavors.

**Sausage and Apple Stuffed Acorn Squash**

Ingredients:

- 2 acorn squash, halved and seeds removed
- 1 tablespoon olive oil
- Salt and pepper to taste
- 1 pound (450g) Italian sausage, casings removed
- 1 onion, diced
- 2 cloves garlic, minced
- 2 apples, cored and diced (such as Granny Smith or Honeycrisp)
- 1/2 cup dried cranberries or raisins
- 1/2 cup chopped pecans or walnuts
- 1 teaspoon dried sage
- 1/2 teaspoon dried thyme
- 1/4 teaspoon ground cinnamon
- 1/4 teaspoon ground nutmeg
- 1/4 cup chopped fresh parsley (optional, for garnish)

Instructions:

Preheat your oven to 400°F (200°C).

Drizzle the cut sides of the acorn squash halves with olive oil and season with salt and pepper. Place them cut side down on a baking sheet lined with parchment paper.

Roast the acorn squash in the preheated oven for 25-30 minutes, or until they are tender when pierced with a fork.

While the squash is roasting, heat a skillet over medium heat. Add the Italian sausage and cook, breaking it up with a spoon, until it is browned and cooked through, about 5-7 minutes.

Add the diced onion to the skillet with the sausage and cook for 2-3 minutes, until the onion is softened and translucent.

Stir in the minced garlic and cook for another minute, until fragrant.

Add the diced apples, dried cranberries or raisins, chopped pecans or walnuts, dried sage, dried thyme, ground cinnamon, and ground nutmeg to the skillet. Stir to combine and cook for 2-3 minutes, until the apples are softened.

Once the acorn squash halves are done roasting, remove them from the oven and flip them over so the cut side is facing up.

Spoon the sausage and apple mixture into the cavities of the acorn squash halves, dividing it evenly among them.

Return the stuffed acorn squash halves to the oven and bake for an additional 15-20 minutes, or until the filling is heated through and the tops are golden brown.

Once done, remove the stuffed acorn squash from the oven and let them cool for a few minutes before serving.

Garnish with chopped fresh parsley, if desired, before serving.

Enjoy the savory and sweet flavors of this delicious sausage and apple stuffed acorn squash—it's a hearty and satisfying dish that's perfect for a cozy dinner!

**Creamy Polenta**

Ingredients:

- 4 cups water or broth (vegetable or chicken)
- 1 cup polenta (cornmeal)
- 1 teaspoon salt
- 2 tablespoons unsalted butter
- 1/2 cup grated Parmesan cheese (optional)
- Freshly ground black pepper to taste

Instructions:

In a large saucepan, bring the water or broth to a boil over medium-high heat. Gradually whisk in the polenta in a slow, steady stream, stirring constantly to prevent lumps from forming.

Reduce the heat to low and add the salt. Stir the polenta frequently to prevent it from sticking to the bottom of the pan.

Cook the polenta over low heat, stirring often, until it thickens and becomes creamy, about 20-30 minutes. The polenta should be smooth and creamy in texture.

Once the polenta is cooked to your desired consistency, remove it from the heat. Stir in the unsalted butter until melted and well combined. This will add richness to the polenta.

If using, stir in the grated Parmesan cheese until melted and incorporated into the polenta.

Season the creamy polenta with freshly ground black pepper to taste.

Serve the creamy polenta hot as a side dish or as a base for your favorite toppings.

Enjoy the creamy and comforting texture of this delicious polenta recipe! It pairs well with roasted vegetables, braised meats, or sautéed mushrooms.

**Roasted Vegetable Lasagna**

Ingredients:

- 9 lasagna noodles
- 2 tablespoons olive oil
- 2 cups diced vegetables (such as bell peppers, zucchini, eggplant, mushrooms, and onions)
- 3 cloves garlic, minced
- 1 (24-ounce) jar marinara sauce
- 1 (15-ounce) container ricotta cheese
- 1 cup shredded mozzarella cheese
- 1/2 cup grated Parmesan cheese
- 1/4 cup chopped fresh basil or parsley
- Salt and pepper to taste

Instructions:

Preheat your oven to 400°F (200°C). Grease a 9x13-inch baking dish with olive oil or non-stick cooking spray.

Cook the lasagna noodles according to the package instructions until al dente. Drain and set aside.

Heat the olive oil in a large skillet over medium heat. Add the diced vegetables and minced garlic to the skillet. Cook, stirring occasionally, until the vegetables are tender and lightly browned, about 8-10 minutes. Season with salt and pepper to taste.

Spread a thin layer of marinara sauce on the bottom of the prepared baking dish. Place three lasagna noodles on top of the marinara sauce, overlapping slightly to cover the bottom of the dish.

Spread half of the ricotta cheese evenly over the noodles.

Spoon half of the roasted vegetables over the ricotta cheese.

Sprinkle half of the shredded mozzarella cheese and grated Parmesan cheese over the vegetables.

Repeat the layers: marinara sauce, lasagna noodles, remaining ricotta cheese, remaining roasted vegetables, and remaining shredded mozzarella cheese and grated Parmesan cheese.

Cover the baking dish with aluminum foil and bake in the preheated oven for 25-30 minutes.

Remove the foil and continue baking for an additional 10-15 minutes, or until the cheese is melted and bubbly and the lasagna is heated through.

Once done, remove the roasted vegetable lasagna from the oven and let it cool for a few minutes before slicing.
Garnish with chopped fresh basil or parsley before serving.

Enjoy the delicious and wholesome flavors of this roasted vegetable lasagna—it's a satisfying and nutritious meal that's sure to please everyone at the table!

**Cinnamon Baked Apples**

Ingredients:

- 4 large apples (such as Granny Smith or Honeycrisp)
- 1/4 cup brown sugar, packed
- 1 teaspoon ground cinnamon
- 1/4 teaspoon ground nutmeg
- 2 tablespoons unsalted butter, cut into small cubes
- 1/2 cup water
- Vanilla ice cream or whipped cream for serving (optional)

Instructions:

Preheat your oven to 375°F (190°C). Grease a baking dish large enough to hold the apples.

Wash the apples and remove the cores using an apple corer or a small knife, leaving the bottoms intact.

In a small bowl, mix together the brown sugar, ground cinnamon, and ground nutmeg.

Place the cored apples in the prepared baking dish. If necessary, trim a thin slice from the bottom of each apple to help them stand upright.

Stuff each apple cavity with the brown sugar and cinnamon mixture, dividing it evenly among the apples.

Place a few cubes of butter on top of each stuffed apple.

Pour the water into the bottom of the baking dish around the apples. This will help keep the apples moist while they bake.

Cover the baking dish with aluminum foil and bake in the preheated oven for 30-40 minutes, or until the apples are tender when pierced with a fork.

Remove the foil and bake for an additional 5-10 minutes, or until the apples are caramelized and golden brown on top.

Once done, remove the baked apples from the oven and let them cool for a few minutes before serving.

Serve the cinnamon baked apples warm, optionally topped with a scoop of vanilla ice cream or a dollop of whipped cream.

Enjoy the warm and comforting flavors of these delicious cinnamon baked apples!

These cinnamon baked apples are perfect for a cozy dessert on a chilly evening. They're simple to make and full of warm, comforting flavors that everyone will love.

**Potato Leek Soup**

Ingredients:

- 2 tablespoons unsalted butter
- 2 leeks, white and light green parts only, sliced
- 3 cloves garlic, minced
- 4 cups chicken or vegetable broth
- 4 large potatoes, peeled and diced
- 1 teaspoon dried thyme
- Salt and pepper to taste
- 1 cup heavy cream or half-and-half
- Chopped fresh chives or parsley for garnish (optional)

Instructions:

In a large pot or Dutch oven, melt the butter over medium heat.
Add the sliced leeks to the pot and cook, stirring occasionally, until softened, about 5-7 minutes.
Add the minced garlic to the pot and cook for another minute, until fragrant.
Pour the chicken or vegetable broth into the pot and bring it to a simmer.
Add the diced potatoes and dried thyme to the pot. Season with salt and pepper to taste.
Cover the pot and simmer the soup for 15-20 minutes, or until the potatoes are tender when pierced with a fork.
Once the potatoes are cooked, use an immersion blender to puree the soup until smooth and creamy. Alternatively, you can transfer the soup in batches to a blender and blend until smooth, then return it to the pot.
Stir in the heavy cream or half-and-half until well combined. Adjust the seasoning with additional salt and pepper if needed.
Heat the soup over low heat until warmed through, but do not boil.
Once heated through, remove the soup from the heat and ladle it into bowls.
Garnish each bowl of potato leek soup with chopped fresh chives or parsley, if desired.
Serve the potato leek soup hot with crusty bread or a side salad.

Enjoy the creamy and flavorful goodness of this delicious potato leek soup—it's sure to warm you up on a cold day!

**Stuffed Pork Tenderloin with Cranberry Sauce**

Ingredients:

For the stuffed pork tenderloin:

- 2 pork tenderloins (about 1 to 1 1/2 pounds each)
- Salt and pepper to taste
- 1 tablespoon olive oil
- 2 cups baby spinach leaves
- 1 cup crumbled goat cheese (or feta cheese)
- 1/2 cup dried cranberries
- 1/4 cup chopped walnuts or pecans (optional)
- 2 tablespoons chopped fresh sage or rosemary

For the cranberry sauce:

- 1 cup fresh or frozen cranberries
- 1/2 cup orange juice
- 1/4 cup honey or maple syrup
- 1 teaspoon grated orange zest
- 1/2 teaspoon ground cinnamon
- Pinch of salt

Instructions:

For the stuffed pork tenderloin:

Preheat your oven to 375°F (190°C). Grease a baking dish with olive oil or non-stick cooking spray.

Butterfly the pork tenderloins by making a lengthwise cut down the center of each tenderloin, being careful not to cut all the way through. Open the tenderloins like a book and pound them gently to flatten to an even thickness. Season the inside and outside of the tenderloins with salt and pepper.

In a large skillet, heat the olive oil over medium heat. Add the baby spinach leaves and cook until wilted, about 2-3 minutes. Remove the spinach from the skillet and set aside.

In the same skillet, add the crumbled goat cheese (or feta cheese), dried cranberries, chopped nuts (if using), and chopped fresh sage or rosemary. Cook for 1-2 minutes, stirring, until the cheese is slightly melted and the ingredients are well combined.

Spread the cheese and cranberry mixture evenly over the inside of each butterflied pork tenderloin. Top with the cooked spinach.

Roll up each tenderloin tightly, starting from the long side, and secure with kitchen twine at 1-inch intervals.

Place the stuffed pork tenderloins in the prepared baking dish. Drizzle with a little olive oil and season with additional salt and pepper, if desired.

Roast in the preheated oven for 25-30 minutes, or until the internal temperature reaches 145°F (63°C) for medium-rare or 160°F (71°C) for medium, as measured with a meat thermometer inserted into the thickest part of the tenderloins.

Once done, remove the stuffed pork tenderloins from the oven and let them rest for 5 minutes before slicing.

For the cranberry sauce:

While the pork tenderloins are roasting, make the cranberry sauce. In a small saucepan, combine the cranberries, orange juice, honey or maple syrup, grated orange zest, ground cinnamon, and a pinch of salt.

Bring the mixture to a boil over medium-high heat, then reduce the heat to low and simmer for 10-15 minutes, stirring occasionally, until the cranberries burst and the sauce thickens slightly.

Once done, remove the cranberry sauce from the heat and let it cool slightly before serving.

To serve:

Slice the stuffed pork tenderloins into rounds and arrange them on a serving platter.

Serve the sliced pork tenderloin with the cranberry sauce on the side.

Garnish with additional fresh herbs, if desired.

Enjoy the delicious combination of flavors in this stuffed pork tenderloin with cranberry sauce—it's a festive and impressive dish that's sure to wow your guests!

**Roasted Beet Salad with Goat Cheese**

Ingredients:

- 3-4 medium beets, preferably a mix of red and golden beets
- 2 tablespoons olive oil
- Salt and pepper to taste
- 4 cups mixed salad greens (such as arugula, spinach, or mixed baby greens)
- 4 ounces goat cheese, crumbled
- 1/4 cup chopped walnuts or pecans (optional)
- 2 tablespoons balsamic vinegar
- 1 tablespoon honey or maple syrup
- 1 teaspoon Dijon mustard
- 1/4 cup extra virgin olive oil
- Salt and pepper to taste

Instructions:

Preheat your oven to 400°F (200°C). Wash the beets and trim off any tops and roots.

Place the beets on a large piece of aluminum foil. Drizzle them with olive oil and sprinkle with salt and pepper. Wrap the foil around the beets to form a packet.

Roast the beets in the preheated oven for 45-60 minutes, or until they are tender when pierced with a fork. The cooking time will depend on the size of the beets.

Let the beets cool slightly, then peel off the skins using your fingers or a paper towel. Cut the beets into wedges or slices.

While the beets are roasting, prepare the vinaigrette. In a small bowl, whisk together the balsamic vinegar, honey or maple syrup, Dijon mustard, and extra virgin olive oil until emulsified. Season with salt and pepper to taste.

Arrange the mixed salad greens on a serving platter or individual plates.

Top the salad greens with the roasted beet slices or wedges.

Sprinkle the crumbled goat cheese and chopped walnuts or pecans (if using) over the beets.

Drizzle the balsamic vinaigrette over the salad.

Serve the roasted beet salad immediately, while the beets are still warm, or chill it in the refrigerator for a cold salad.

Enjoy the vibrant colors and delicious flavors of this roasted beet salad with goat cheese!

This salad makes a wonderful appetizer or side dish for any meal. The combination of sweet roasted beets, tangy goat cheese, and flavorful vinaigrette is sure to impress your guests.

**Garlic and Herb Roasted Prime Rib**

Ingredients:

- 1 (4 to 6-pound) bone-in prime rib roast
- 6 cloves garlic, minced
- 2 tablespoons chopped fresh rosemary
- 2 tablespoons chopped fresh thyme
- 2 tablespoons chopped fresh parsley
- 2 tablespoons olive oil
- Salt and pepper to taste
- 1 cup beef broth or red wine (optional)

Instructions:

Remove the prime rib roast from the refrigerator and let it sit at room temperature for about 1 hour before cooking. This will help it cook more evenly.
Preheat your oven to 450°F (230°C).
In a small bowl, combine the minced garlic, chopped fresh rosemary, thyme, parsley, and olive oil to make the herb rub.
Pat the prime rib roast dry with paper towels. Season the roast generously with salt and pepper on all sides.
Rub the herb mixture all over the surface of the prime rib roast, coating it evenly.
Place the seasoned prime rib roast, bone-side down, in a roasting pan or on a rack set inside a roasting pan.
Roast the prime rib in the preheated oven for 15 minutes to sear the outside.
Reduce the oven temperature to 325°F (160°C) and continue roasting the prime rib until it reaches your desired level of doneness, about 15 minutes per pound for medium-rare (a meat thermometer inserted into the thickest part of the roast should read 135°F (57°C) for medium-rare).
If desired, you can add beef broth or red wine to the bottom of the roasting pan to help keep the meat moist and add flavor to the drippings.
Once the prime rib roast reaches the desired doneness, remove it from the oven and tent it loosely with aluminum foil. Let it rest for at least 15-20 minutes before carving to allow the juices to redistribute.
To serve, slice the prime rib roast against the grain into thick slices. Serve it with your favorite side dishes and enjoy!

This garlic and herb roasted prime rib is sure to be the centerpiece of your holiday table or special dinner. The flavorful herb crust and tender, juicy meat will impress your guests and make for a memorable meal.

**Winter Vegetable Tian**

Ingredients:

- 2 tablespoons olive oil
- 2 cloves garlic, minced
- 1 onion, thinly sliced
- 2 medium potatoes, thinly sliced
- 2 medium sweet potatoes, thinly sliced
- 2 carrots, thinly sliced
- 2 parsnips, thinly sliced
- 1 small butternut squash, peeled, seeded, and thinly sliced
- Salt and pepper to taste
- 2 tablespoons chopped fresh herbs (such as thyme, rosemary, or sage)
- 1/2 cup grated Parmesan cheese (optional)

Instructions:

Preheat your oven to 375°F (190°C).
Heat the olive oil in a large skillet over medium heat. Add the minced garlic and sliced onion to the skillet and cook until softened, about 3-4 minutes.
Arrange the thinly sliced vegetables in overlapping layers in a greased baking dish or cast-iron skillet, alternating the types of vegetables. You can arrange them in rows or concentric circles, depending on the shape of your dish.
Season the layered vegetables with salt, pepper, and chopped fresh herbs.
Cover the baking dish or skillet with aluminum foil and bake in the preheated oven for 30-40 minutes, or until the vegetables are tender when pierced with a fork.
Remove the foil and sprinkle the grated Parmesan cheese (if using) over the top of the vegetables.
Return the uncovered tian to the oven and bake for an additional 10-15 minutes, or until the cheese is melted and golden brown.
Once done, remove the winter vegetable tian from the oven and let it cool for a few minutes before serving.
Serve the winter vegetable tian hot as a side dish or vegetarian main course.

Enjoy the beautiful presentation and delicious flavors of this winter vegetable tian—it's sure to be a hit at your next gathering or holiday meal! Feel free to customize the vegetables and herbs based on what's in season and your personal preferences.

**Chocolate Peppermint Trifle**

Ingredients:

- 1 box of chocolate cake mix (plus ingredients needed to prepare the cake, such as eggs, oil, and water)
- 1 cup heavy cream
- 8 ounces cream cheese, softened
- 1/2 cup powdered sugar
- 1 teaspoon peppermint extract
- Crushed candy canes or peppermint candies
- Chocolate syrup or hot fudge sauce
- Optional: chocolate shavings or curls for garnish

Instructions:

Prepare the chocolate cake according to the instructions on the box. Once baked and cooled, cut the cake into cubes.
In a large bowl, beat the heavy cream until stiff peaks form.
In another bowl, beat the softened cream cheese and powdered sugar until smooth and creamy. Add the peppermint extract and mix until combined.
Gently fold the whipped cream into the cream cheese mixture until well combined.
To assemble the trifle, start by layering half of the chocolate cake cubes in the bottom of a trifle dish or large glass bowl.
Drizzle some chocolate syrup or hot fudge sauce over the cake cubes.
Spread half of the cream cheese and whipped cream mixture over the cake layer.
Sprinkle a layer of crushed candy canes or peppermint candies over the cream cheese layer.
Repeat the layers with the remaining chocolate cake cubes, chocolate syrup, cream cheese mixture, and crushed candy canes.
Cover the trifle dish with plastic wrap and refrigerate for at least 2 hours, or overnight, to allow the flavors to meld and the dessert to set.
Before serving, garnish the top of the trifle with chocolate shavings or curls, if desired.
Serve the chocolate peppermint trifle chilled and enjoy the delicious combination of chocolate and peppermint flavors!

This chocolate peppermint trifle is sure to be a crowd-pleaser at any holiday gathering or special occasion. It's rich, creamy, and filled with festive flavors that everyone will love.

www.ingramcontent.com/pod-product-compliance
Lightning Source LLC
LaVergne TN
LVHW081611060526
838201LV00054B/2205